The Garden Journal

the essentials

Liane Doxey

DEDICATION

To everyone that has enjoyed my hand bound journals,
I hope you are pleased with this published version.

And to my parents, your encouragement and enthusiasm
has meant everything to me.
Thank you so much.

CONTENTS

ACKNOWLEDGMENTS

Thank you to all of the wonderful people that are so quotable and
I felt I must include in this book. They are Gertrude Jekyll, Paul James,
Anatole France, Ursula K. LeGuin, Claude Monet and Albert Schweitzer.

The fonts used in this book are from Tahoma and Californian FB
and also css Hand from Stamp'in Up.

Reference
& Planning

supplies

Seed Starting:

- ○   ○
- ○   ○
- ○   ○
- ○   ○
- ○   ○
- ○   ○
- ○   ○
- ○   ○

Fertilizers:

- ○   ○
- ○   ○
- ○   ○
- ○   ○
- ○   ○
- ○   ○

Tools:

- ○   ○
- ○   ○
- ○   ○
- ○   ○

needed

string, supports....::

- ○
- ○
- ○
- ○
- ○
- ○
- ○

- ○
- ○
- ○
- ○
- ○
- ○
- ○

pots, furniture...:

- ○
- ○
- ○
- ○
- ○
- ○

- ○
- ○
- ○
- ○
- ○
- ○

other:

- ○
- ○
- ○
- ○

- ○
- ○
- ○
- ○

Liane Doxey

plants & combinations

To know is nothing at all...

to try this year

plant □□□□□□□□□□□□□□ size □□□□□□□□□□□□□□□□□□ garden location □□□□□□□□□□□□□□ from

to imagine is everything.   *-Anatole France*

annuals

○ ....

○ ....

○ ....

○ ....

○ ....

○ ....

○ ....

○ ....

○ ....

○ ....

○ ....

○ ....

○ ....

List the annuals purchased this year and note how you liked them.
Are they worth repeating?
Would you do something differently with them next year?
This will be a great place to refer back to next year when planning purchases.

○

○

○

○

○

○

○

○

○

○

○

○

○
_____

○
_____

○
_____

○
_____

○
_____

○
_____

○
_____

○
_____

○
_____

○
_____

○
_____

○
_____

○
_____

○
_____

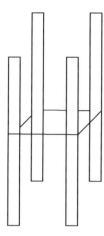

Stake & Support Early

Provide support to tall and top heavy plants. This can help keep your plants healthy, safer from wind breakage and makes such a difference visually. Install stakes and cages while the plants can be controlled. This is also essential for having the support hidden by the time the plant is full grown. I get so caught up in a plants progress that I often forget to put supports in early. As a result I like creating a list of my plants as a reminder and I also note the type of support and the date I staked them as a reference for next year. I'll admit that in August I am often adding a few plants to the list to remind me to stake them next year.

There are many types of supports that include wire cages or simply placing a stick in the ground and attaching the stem to it with string or a small strip of panty hose. You can create a box shaped support of string and sticks (see above). Experiment and choose the one that will be strong enough to support yet still able to blend into the plants growth.

○   ○

○   ○

○   ○

○   ○

○   ○

○   ○

○   ○

○   ○

divide & conquer

For optimal health and blooming, dividing plants are often required. The general rule of thumb is spring flowering plants should be divided in fall and fall flowering plants divided in the spring. If in doubt, divide in the spring. This seems to be the best time for many of us because the ground is still soft which makes it easier for the divided plants roots to take hold and acclimate. And let's face it, we are more likely to baby a plant in the spring versus the end of summer when we tend to have the survival of the fittest attitude. Do try to avoid dividing in the heat of summer when plants are using all of their energy to simply survive. You'll have far fewer casualties this way.

How do you know it's time to divide? Often if a plant has significantly fewer blooms than it had the previous year or if it forms a halo effect in the center of the plant, it's time to dig up and divide.

Keep a list of plants you divided this year or perhaps list the plants you want to remember to divide next year.

○

○

○

○

○

○

○

○

○

○

○

container gardening

Containers are a great way to have continuous blooms in the garden and create just the right ambience at an entrance or seating area.

Below, note the plants you have used in a container and how well you liked them.   Be sure to clean your vessels well before planting. You don't want to transfer any potential fungus or disease to your new planting.

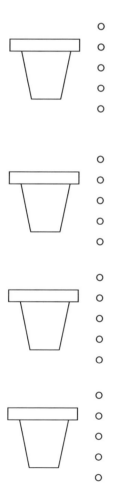

Liane Doxey

Starting by Seed

The wise gardener anticipates June in January.

Starting plants by seed is magical. It can also save you phenomenal amounts of money. I now grow most of my annuals by seed and all of my vegetables. There is nothing like putting a seed in earth and watching it grow - it's amazing.

In this section you will find:

Seeds to Purchase:
Here you can create your wish list of seeds you are considering or ones you will definitely be purchasing. It's so helpful to have a reference of which purveyors carry the seeds you may be looking for. Be sure to use the column devoted to where you may plant them. This may help you narrow down your list if you realize you have nowhere to go with it!

Seed Starting Chart:
- Where You Purchased the Seed- for reordering this in invaluable and will also provide an indication if you want to purchase from that purveyor again, based upon the results of your yield.
- Planting Particulars such as date, how many seeds you planted, the type of soil (brands of seed starting mix, enriched soil, etc.), what you planted in such as a peat pot, a plastic cup, directly in the garden, etc.
- Germination and Transplant Particulars- this will tell you how viable each seed was. This is a great resource for next year's plans of who to buy from, if you want to try that seed again, it will also tell you if the growing conditions may have been a factor.
- Notes – where you planted the seedlings, include when the plants bloomed, when vegetables were harvested, how successful was it, would you try them again next year, etc.

seeds to purchase

Seed	Purveyor	Where to Plant

seeds to purchase

Seed	Purveyor	Where to Plant

seeds to purchase

Seed	Purveyor	Where to Plant

seed starting chart

seed, purveyor, purchase date		
Date planted	Germinate date	Notes: planting date, bloom date, harvest date, how well did they do? Will you grow it again?
Soil type	Transplant date	
# of seeds	# of plants	
In what		

seed starting chart

seed starting chart

seed, purveyor, purchase date		
Date planted	Germinate date	Notes: planting date, bloom date, harvest date, how well did they do? Will you grow it again?
Soil type	Transplant date	
# of seeds	# of plants	
In what		

seed starting chart

seed starting chart

seed, purveyor, purchase date		
Date planted	Germinate date	Notes: planting date, bloom date, harvest date, how well did they do? will you grow it again?
Soil type	Transplant date	
# of seeds	# of plants	
In what		

seed starting chart

seed starting chart

seed, purveyor, purchase date		
Date planted	Germinate date	Notes: planting date, bloom date, harvest date, how well did they do? Will you grow it again?
Soil type	Transplant date	
# of seeds	# of plants	
In what		

seed starting chart

seed starting chart

seed, purveyor, purchase date		
Date planted	Germinate date	Notes: planting date, bloom date, harvest date, how well did they do? Will you grow it again?
Soil type	Transplant date	
# of seeds	# of plants	
In what		

seed starting chart

In Bloom

I perhaps owe having become a painter to flowers.
- Claude Monet

When a plant is blooming is valuable information.   Below are the primary ways I have used this section. I'm sure you will find plenty more.

- Where to plant new additions to the garden. For example, when purchasing a new plant in September, which will bloom in May, all you need to do is refer back to this list of what was in bloom in May to decide where your new plant will look its best.
- Referring to this section the following year is great because you can watch a plants growth to determine when to anticipate its blooms or you will be able to track how weather conditions may be affecting their progress.
- This record may be able to provide clues when it is time to divide the plant to rejuvenate it. Dividing plants are a perfect way to expand your garden or share part of your garden with a friend.

Just sit down in your garden once a week and update. It's fun and it gives you an instant feeling of pride and accomplishment!

Start Bloom	The Plant	End Bloom

Liane Doxey

Start Bloom	The Plant	End Bloom

Start Bloom	The Plant	End Bloom

Start Bloom	The Plant	End Bloom

Start Bloom	The Plant	End Bloom

Liane Doxey

Start Bloom	The Plant	End Bloom

Start Bloom	The Plant	End Bloom

Start Bloom	The Plant	End Bloom

Start Bloom	The Plant	End Bloom

Favorite Things

In the hope of reaching for the moon,
Men fail to see the flowers
That blossom at their feet.
-albert schweitzer

In this section list what you loved the most. It could be:

- Favorite plant combinations.
- Recipes for your freshly harvested vegetables.
- Memories of garden parties that never fail to make you smile.
- That perfect morning you watched the sunrise over your garden. Okay, maybe it was a sunset.

- ○
- ○
- ○
- ○
- ○
- ○
- ○
- ○
- ○
- ○
- ○
- ○
- ○
- ○
- ○
- ○
- ○
- ○
- ○

○

○

○

○

○

○

○

○

○

○

○

○

○

○

○

○

○

○

○

○

○

○

○

○

○

○

○

○

○

○

○

○

○

○

○

○

○

○

○

○

○

○

○

○

○

○

○

○

○

○

○

○

○

The Journal

Some of the most important time spent in the garden
is spent not gardening.
– Paul James

This is the area where you can record anything your heart desires.   Certainly you can keep a record of date and temperature but there are so many other things you will want to remember. Below are a few ideas.

- What you feel when you see the first lightning bugs of the season floating among your flowers.
- Butterflies you've never seen before.
- When you see the first signs of life from specific plants. This is a wonderful reference for you the following year as you are eagerly anticipating their return.
- It's a great place to record projects, such as when and where you planted bulbs that may not bloom for another year or experiments noting what you want to modify or repeat next year.
- I tend to record more general weather conditions, such as early heat waves, late frosts, drought conditions...anything that may affect this years and potentially the next season's growth.

I've often found myself reading last year's journal entries during the long winter months to give me something to dream about and anticipate. What would you like to remember?

date

date

date

date

date

date

date

date

date

date

date

date

date

date

date

Liane Doxey

date

66

date

date

date

date

date

date

date

Liane Doxey

Just
Imagine

It is good to have an end to journey toward,
But it is the journey that matters most in the end.
-Ursula k. LeGuin

Most gardeners plan to make changes to their garden. This is the spot to record your brainstorming.

This section is in a graph formation so you can draw plots of earth and list options. Be sure to include landmarks such as the garage, air conditioners, trees, etc. Each sheet in this section can represent an area you would like to develop. This sort of brainstorming may go on for months so I recommend using pencil. You're only limited by your imagination.

This section is also a perfect spot to simply record what is currently planted in your garden. An easy reference of what plant is coming up in spring and even a record to ensure you properly rotate your vegetable beds. Each year after bulb planting, I record their names and where it was placed in the garden. Once up, those daffodils look remarkably similar and somehow we tend to have very high expectations of our memories in the spring. This record will help you out.

just imagine...

The area of my garden:

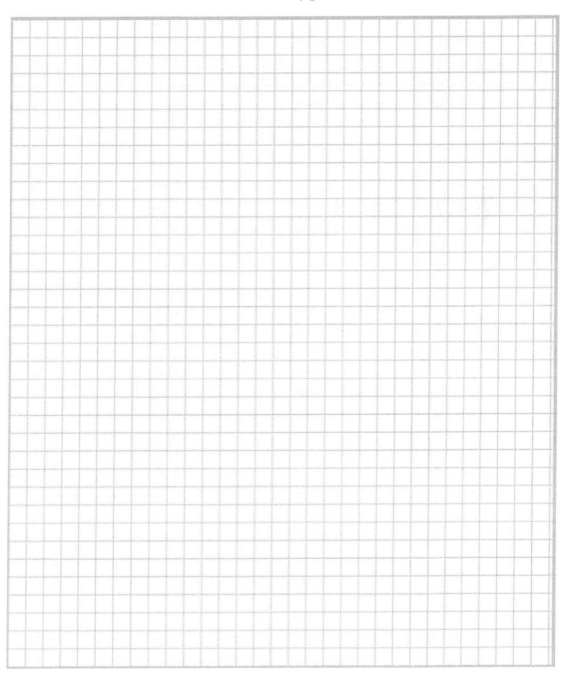

just imagine...

The area of my garden:

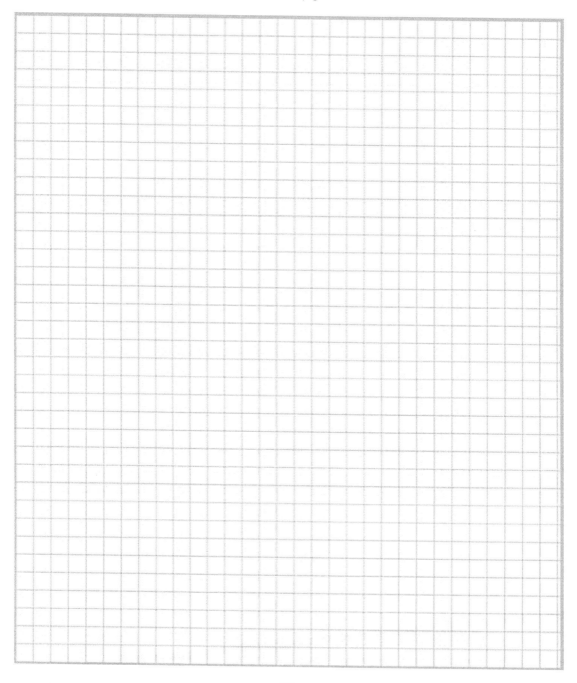

just imagine...

The area of my garden:

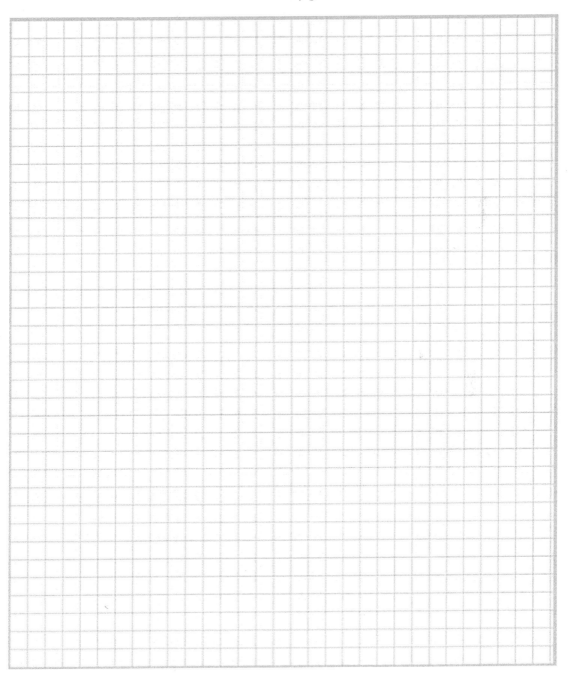

just imagine...

The area of my garden:

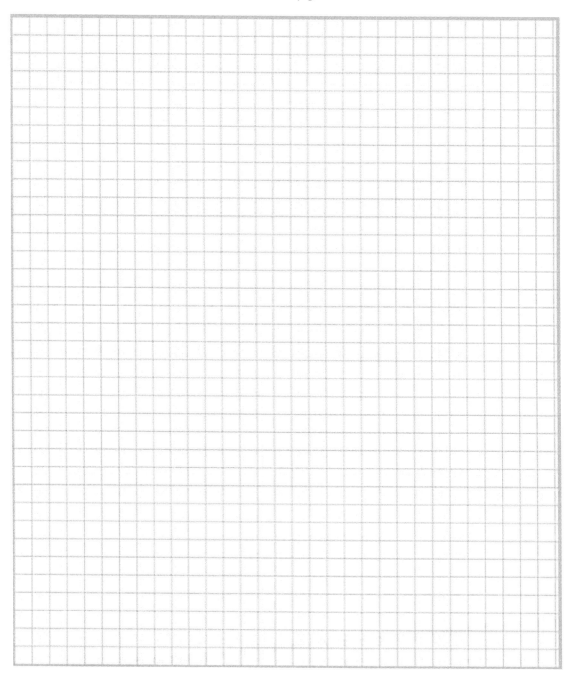

just imagine...

The area of my garden:

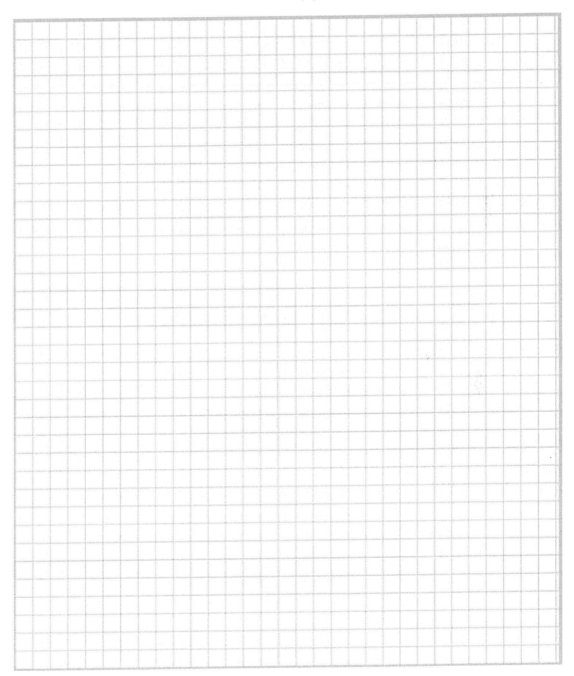

just imagine...

The area of my garden:

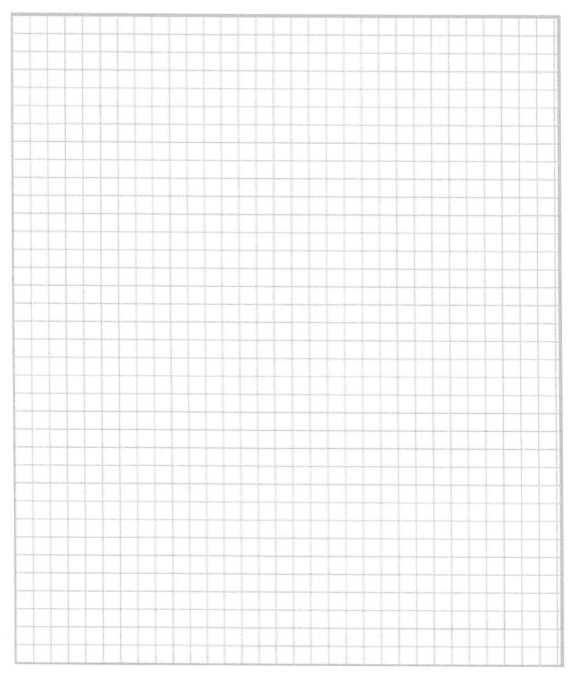

just imagine...

The area of my garden:

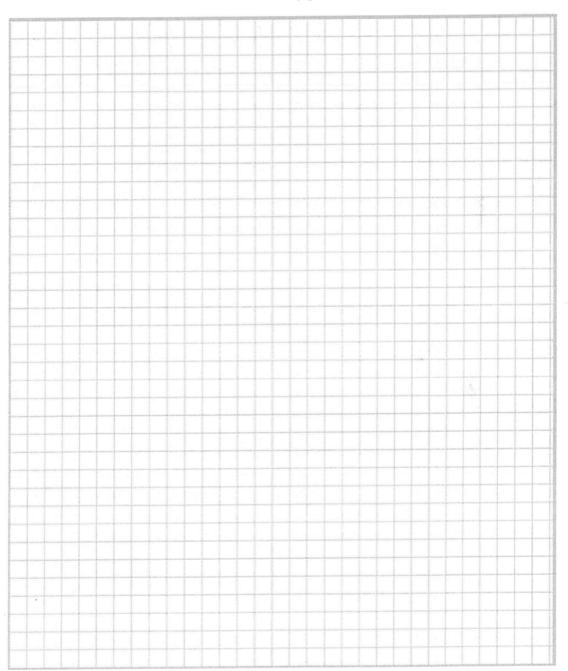

Liane Doxey

just imagine...

The area of my garde:

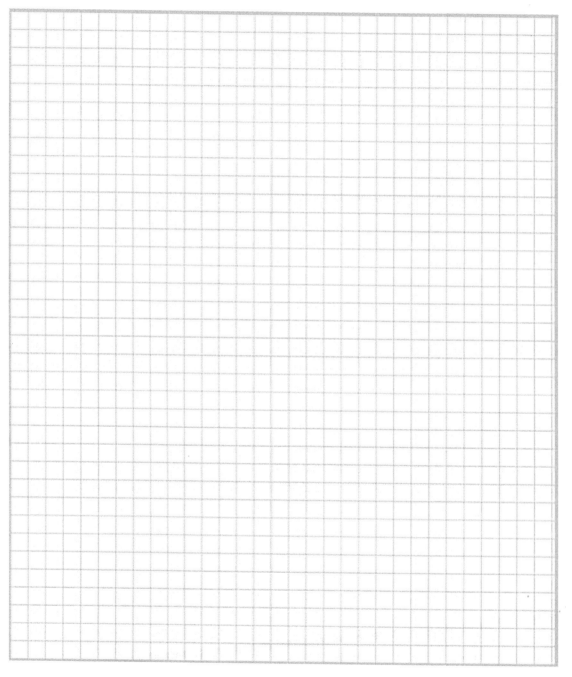

just imagine...

The area of my garden::

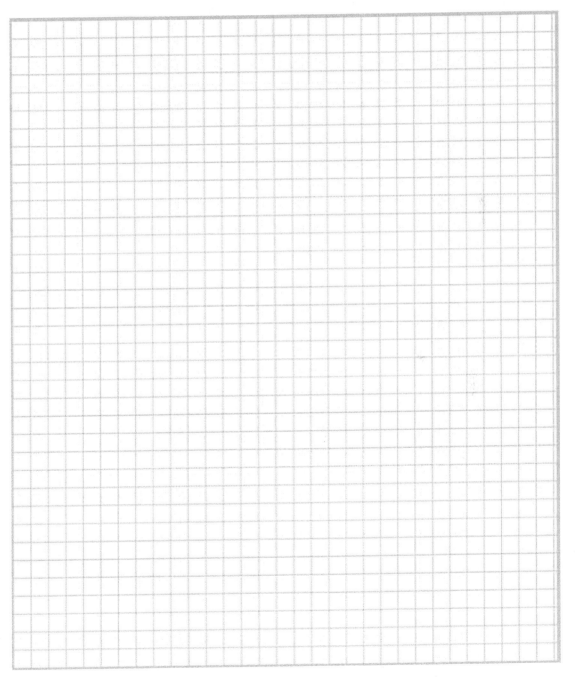

just imagine...

The area of my garden:

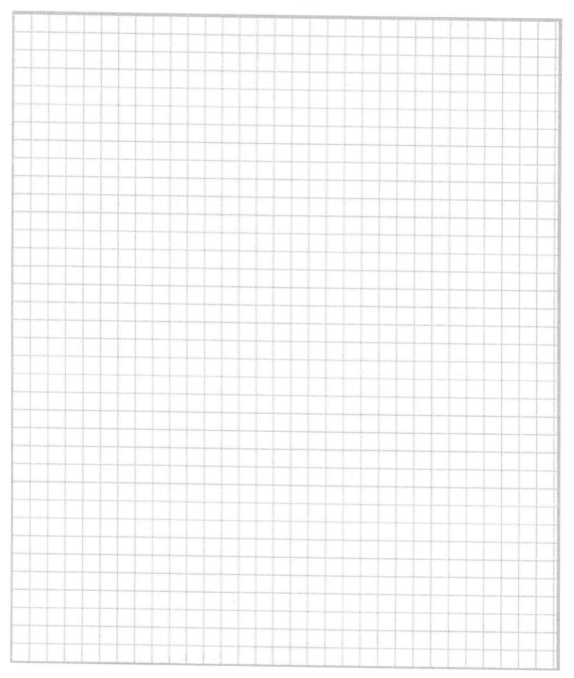

just imagine...

The area of my garden:

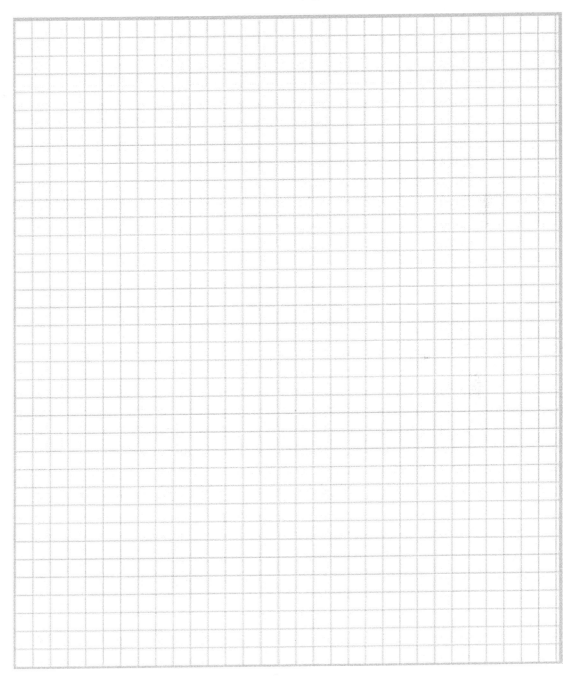

Purchases

A society grows great
when old men plant trees
whose shade they know
they shall never sit in.
-Greek proverb

Record the plants and supplies you purchased, what they cost and where you purchased them. Once, I found my grandmothers records and marveled at what she could buy for a nickel.

This is a great reference so you can advise curious friends where you found a particular plant. For personal favorites you will easily be able to go back for more the next year or even see a trend of nurseries that seem to supply your best success stories so you can be sure to frequent that shop. It's also not a bad budgeting technique as it can tell you where all your money went!

purchases

date	from	what	price

purchases

date	from	what	price

purchases

date	from	what	price

purchases

date	from	what	price

purchases

date	from	what	price

purchases

date	from	what	price

purchases

date	from	what	price

The love of gardening is a seed,
once sown, never dies.
-Gertrude Jekyll

26908180R00062

Made in the USA
San Bernardino, CA
05 December 2015